What Is Justification by Faith Alone?

Basics of the Faith

Sean Michael Lucas, Series Editor

What Is Justification by Faith Alone?

J. V. Fesko

P&R
PUBLISHING
P.O.BOX 817 • PHILLIPSBURG • NEW JERSEY 08865-0817

Page design by Tobias Design

Printed in the United States of America

Library of Congress Cataloging-in-Publication Data

Fesko, J. V., 1970–
   What is justification by faith alone? / J. V. Fesko.
      p. cm. — (Basics of the reformed faith)
   Includes bibliographical references.
   ISBN 978-1-59638-083-7 (pbk.)
   1.   Justification (Christian theology) 2.   Reformed Church—Doctrines.
I. Title.
  BT764.3.F47 2008
  234'.7—dc22

                                   2007038778

INTRODUCTION

■Ever since Martin Luther, the famous sixteenth-century Reformer, nailed his ninety-five theses to the castle door of Wittenberg, the doctrine of justification by faith alone has been one of the great truths of the Reformed faith. During the sixteenth century the Protestant Reformers had five rallying points of belief: Scripture alone (*sola Scriptura*), Christ alone (*solus Christus*), grace alone (*sola gratia*), faith alone (*sola fide*), and to the glory of God alone (*soli Deo Gloria*). It is particularly three of these slogans that are of great significance for the doctrine of justification. Before we proceed, we should first define what we mean by the phrase the doctrine of justification by faith alone.

All people must at some point in their existence stand in the presence of God and be judged. There are two possible outcomes, either a guilty or not-guilty verdict. Or, in biblical terms, God will either condemn or justify the person who stands before him. In order for God to justify a person, he requires absolute perfect righteousness, that is, obedience to his law. Man, however, is sinful and lies under the curse of God. How can sinful man walk away from God's judgment with anything but a guilty verdict? The answer comes in the doctrine of justification by faith alone. The Westminster Shorter Catechism, originally written in the seventeenth century and now one of the catechisms for most conservative Presbyterian denominations, defines justification as: "An act of God's free grace, wherein he pardons all our sins, and accepts us as righteous in his sight, only for the righteousness of Christ imputed to us, and received by faith alone" (Q. 33). Here we see the basics of the doctrine of justification by faith alone.

How can a sinner be justified in the sight of God? He can only be justified if another man stands in his place and offers the perfect obedience, or righteousness, that God requires. This is what Jesus has done for the one who looks to him by faith. Jesus lived on behalf of sinners. In other words, throughout his life Jesus was perfectly and completely obedient to the will and law of his heavenly Father. Jesus also suffered the penalty of sin throughout his earthly life, which culminated in his crucifixion on the cross. This means that Jesus both suffered the penalty of the law and offers his perfect obedience to those who look to him by faith. And Jesus was raised from the dead, which signaled that his perfect sacrifice was accepted by the Father, securing the victory over sin and death. The sinner contributes nothing to his justification, to this verdict that God renders. It is for these reasons that the nineteenth-century Scottish theologian and poet, Horatius Bonar, once wrote, "Thy works, not mine, O Christ, speak gladness to this heart; they tell me all is done; they bid my fear depart." Perhaps now the cries of the Reformation begin to make more sense.

It is by God's grace alone (*sola gratia*) that he justifies the sinner. God has every right to condemn the sinner but instead shows him mercy and shows him his grace. Justification is through Christ alone (*solus Christus*), as it is the work of Christ—his life, death, and resurrection—that serves as the judicial basis for the believer's verdict of righteousness. And a sinner is justified by faith alone (*sola fide*). In other words, it is not the obedience or good works of the sinner. Rather, it is that the sinner looks exclusively to the person and work of Christ to receive this verdict of righteousness rather than the verdict of condemnation he deserves. These three points are the basics of the doctrine of justification by faith alone, and it is these points that we want to examine in the following pages so we come to understand this essential truth of the Reformed faith.

John Calvin, the sixteenth-century second-generation Reformer, explained that "unless you first of all grasp what your relationship to God is, and the nature of his judgment concerning you, you have neither a foundation on which to establish your salvation nor one on which to build piety toward God." It was for this reason that Calvin believed that justification was "the main hinge on which religion turns."[1] It is no wonder that a seventeenth-century Reformed theologian, Johann Heinrich Alsted, one of the delegates to the Synod of Dort (1619), which gave us the "five points of Calvinism," would later write that the doctrine of justification is the *articulus stantis et cadentis ecclesiae*, "the article upon which the church stands or falls."

To understand this all-important doctrine, we will first survey the opening chapters of the Bible and the creation of Adam to see how God always intended to create and judge his creation. Second, we will see how in a fallen world, God was pointing to the person and work of his Son throughout the Old Testament, proving that a person could never be justified in God's sight by obedience but only by faith alone in the work of Jesus. Third, we will see how through the life, death, and resurrection of Christ we find the basic building blocks of the doctrine of justification by faith alone. Fourth, we will summarize our findings and show how the Reformed churches have historically expressed this doctrine. And fifth, we will answer some commonly asked questions concerning the doctrine.

IN THE BEGINNING

Most are familiar with the basic plot line of Genesis 1–2: God created the heavens and earth and crowned the creation with man, who was made in his image. God told man not to eat of the tree of knowledge, but man disobeyed the command and plunged the world into sin, death, and the oppressive rule of Satan. What many may not realize, however, is that even in the opening chapters of the Bible we find the doctrine of justification.

When God first created man, male and female, he passed a judgment over his work. God created and then declared that everything was "good." In fact, when he created man, the only creature who bore his image, God declared that man was "very good" (Gen. 1:31). God's declaration that he made man "very good" was a judicial declaration. If we recall the conversation between the rich young ruler and Jesus, the Lord asked the young man why he called him "good," as only God was good (Mark 10:18 // Luke 18:19). In the Proverbs, for example, we read: "So you will walk in the way of the good and keep to the paths of the righteous" (2:20). In this verse, the author uses a synonymous parallelism (a Hebraic poetic structure), stating the same truth in two different ways, which tells us that goodness and righteousness are synonymous. So, when God said that man was "very good," he had essentially declared man to be righteous. At the same time, we should note that while man was righteous, his righteousness was unproven; it was untested.

God made a covenant, an agreement, with Adam. This covenant, like other covenants in the Bible, set forth requirements for obedience. In this covenant Adam had two primary responsibilities. First, God required that Adam refrain from eating from the tree of knowledge. The tree of knowledge, in this regard, was a visual symbol of God's command, a visual symbol of his law. Second, God commanded Adam to fill the earth with the image of God, which Adam would have done with the assistance of the woman through procreation. Adam and the woman would have produced offspring that would have borne the image of God and would have in this way filled the earth with God's glory. Adam was also supposed to subdue the earth. In other words, he was supposed to extend the garden-order of God's dwelling place to the ends of the earth. This was the work that God placed before Adam as well as the test of obedience. Upon the conclusion of his test and labors, God would have declared him righteous. Adam's righteousness would no longer be untested, unproven. Rather, it would be conclusively confirmed that Adam was faithful and obedient to the commands of his heavenly Father. If, on the other hand, Adam was disobedient, God told him quite clearly that he would suffer death (Gen. 2:17). Reformed theologians have historically called the relationship between Adam and God the *covenant of works*, or covenant of life. The Westminster Confession of Faith states: "The first covenant made with man was a covenant of works, wherein life was promised to Adam, and in him to his posterity, upon condition of perfect and personal obedience" (7:2).

Sadly, we all know what happened. Adam and the woman sinned, listening to the voice of the serpent rather than heeding God's command. But God, rather than give the couple the just deserts of their disobedience, was instead merciful. Adam and the woman indeed had to suffer the consequences of their sin. They were cast from the dwelling place of God in the garden. They suffered spiritual and physical death. They were now both incapable of offering God the obedience he required and therefore were doomed to live separated from the benevolent presence of the Lord. God, however, showed the couple mercy and promised them that the seed of the woman would conquer the seed of the serpent. In his curse on the serpent, God said, "I will put enmity between you and the woman, and between your offspring and her offspring; he shall bruise your head, and you shall bruise his heel" (Gen. 3:15). In other words, not only would God send someone to reverse the disastrous and tragic consequences of the fall, but this person would also render to God the obedience that he required from the beginning. In fact, for this reason theologians have historically called Genesis 3:15 the first promise of the gospel. God was no longer dealing with Adam and the woman on the basis of the covenant of works, but now there was an entirely new principle at work. God was dealing with the couple on the basis of grace. Historically, Reformed theologians have called this relationship the *covenant of grace*.

Once again the Westminster divines (a seventeenth-century word for *theologians*) state:

> Man, by his fall, having made himself incapable of life by that covenant, the Lord was pleased to make a second, commonly called the Covenant of Grace, whereby He freely offers unto sinners life and salvation by Jesus Christ, requiring of them faith in Him, that they may be saved; and promising to give unto all those that are ordained unto eternal life His Holy Spirit, to make them willing, and able to believe. (7:3)

That Adam took shelter in the covenant of grace and God's first promise of the gospel is evident in his response. Adam gave his wife a new name; she was no longer called *woman*, but now she was called *Eve*, which means giver of life (Gen. 3:20). In other words, Adam placed his faith in the promise that the seed of the woman would deliver them. Adam looked to Christ by faith. Adam knew, perhaps not in every detail, that it was the work of the seed of the woman that would both free them from the bonds of Satan, sin, and death and restore man's place in God's presence.

Adam's faith was not introspective—he did not look to himself to remedy his sin-fallen predicament. Rather, his faith was *extraspective*—he looked to another, he looked to the seed of the woman. We even see hints in the Genesis narrative that man's sin would be cured, but not simply by restoring him to his position in the garden. Adam and Eve's salvation would be far greater. They would be restored to dwell forever in God's presence, and their nakedness, their shame, would be covered through the shed blood of another. We see suggestions of this in that both Adam and Eve were clothed in animal skins that were provided by God himself (Gen. 3:21). The blood of another had to be shed to allow man to return to the presence of God. Man would never again be naked but would be clothed, clothed in the robe of another, robed in the righteousness of the seed of the woman.

IN THE OLD TESTAMENT

Noah and the Flood

Moving beyond the creation and fall narrative, we find that God's good creation quickly degenerated (Gen. 6:5). God therefore purposed to judge the creation and start over with one righteous man and his family, Noah (Gen. 6:7–8). God instructed Noah to build an ark so that the creation, including Noah's family, might be saved. God returned the creation to its Genesis 1:2 state through the flood—waters covered the earth as they had before. Noah and his family emerged from the ark in the re-created earth, but things quickly unraveled. In events eerily evocative of the fall of

Adam and Eve, Noah also fell into sin. Just as Adam and Eve sinned in the garden by eating the forbidden fruit and discovered that they were naked, resulting in the blessing and cursing of seed, so too Noah sinned in a garden-vineyard by consuming too much of the fruit of the vine, became drunk, and was naked. The account of Noah's fall also ended in the blessing and cursing of seed. If there was any question as to man's ability to please God and offer him the righteousness he required, Noah's descendants removed all doubt by constructing the tower of Babel (Gen. 11:1–9). Man was trying once again, as Adam had done in the garden, to be God.

It is on the heels of the tower of Babel incident that we see a new beginning of sorts. From the ash heap of Babel, God called Abram of the Chaldees: "Now the LORD said to Abram, 'Go from your country and your kindred and your father's house to the land that I will show you. And I will make of you a great nation, and I will bless you and make your name great, so that you will be a blessing. I will bless those who bless you, and him who dishonors you I will curse, and in you all the families of the earth shall be blessed'" (Gen. 12:1–3). This is a decided departure from what has happened before. No longer does God command his servants to multiply and fill the earth as he had done with Adam and Noah (Gen. 1:28; 9:1). Now, instead of a command, God himself has promised that he will fill the earth through Abraham and his descendants. The global extent of God's promise is evident when he says that he will make Abram a great nation and that through Abram all the families of the earth will be blessed. It is important to understand that God's promise to Abraham is a continuation of his promise to Adam and Eve that the seed of the woman would conquer the seed of the serpent. Moreover, we see that God has taken up the failed work of Adam. What Adam and Noah failed to do, God will do through his promise to Abraham. It is for these reasons that the apostle Paul calls Genesis 12:3 the gospel: "And the Scripture, foreseeing that God would justify the Gentiles by faith, preached the gospel beforehand to Abraham, saying, 'In you shall all the nations be blessed'" (Gal. 3:8).

Abraham

Continuing forward in the narrative accounts of the great patriarch, we come upon one of the most crucial passages of Scripture regarding the doctrine of justification by faith alone. God made his promise to Abraham that he would make him a great nation and that he would bless all of the families of the earth through him. Abraham received this promise when he was seventy-five years old (Gen. 12:4). However, as the years passed by, it appeared as though God had forgotten about his promise. But God once again came to Abraham: "Fear not, Abram, I am your shield; your reward shall be very great" (Gen. 15:1). Abraham was dismayed, though, because he had no offspring. Eliezer of Damascus, his hired hand, would be his heir (Gen. 15:2–3). In Abraham's mind, he would die childless. God, however, reassured Abraham of his promise to make him a great nation, saying, "This man shall not be your heir; your very own son shall be your heir. . . . Look toward heaven, and number the stars, if you are able to number them. . . . So shall your offspring be" (Gen. 15:4–5). How did Abraham respond to God's promise, to the reiteration of the gospel, as the apostle Paul has told us?

The Genesis narrative tells us: "And he believed the LORD, and he counted it to him as righteousness" (15:6). This is, to say the least, an amazing statement. It is like a lightning bolt flashing in a small, dark room. First, Abraham believed, placing his faith in the Lord's promise, what Paul calls the gospel. Second, God looked upon Abraham, not as a condemned sinner, but as a righteous man. In terms of the greater testimony of the rest of Scripture, righteousness is something that a person can only achieve through complete and perfect obedience to the entire law of God (Lev. 18:5; Deut. 27–30; Gal. 3:10–14; Rom. 10:5). Yet, Abraham receives this righteous status by looking through faith to the promise of God. Third, Genesis 15:6 tells us that God "counted" Abraham's belief as righteousness. That God counted righteousness to Abraham is significant. To count, credit, or impute righteousness to a person means that this righteousness is alien; it is not native to Abraham. It is here in Genesis 15:6 that we see the doctrine of justification by faith alone, or *sola fide*.

Abraham is not declared righteous because of his obedience. Rather, he is declared righteous by his faith in God's promise alone. We receive confirmation of these conclusions from the apostle Paul's inerrant, infallible, and authoritative commentary on this passage. Paul writes: "What then shall we say was gained by Abraham, our forefather according to the flesh? For if Abraham was justified by works, he has something to boast about, but not before God. For what does the Scripture say? 'Abraham believed God, and it was counted to him as righteousness.' Now to the one who works, his wages are not counted as a gift but as his due. And to the one who does not work but trusts him who justifies the ungodly, his faith is counted as righteousness" (Rom. 4:1–5). In Paul's commentary on Genesis 15:6, the apostle eliminates justification by works, or trying to earn one's salvation through obedience to the law. Rather, justification is by faith alone. This is a theme to which we will return, especially when we consider the life, death, and resurrection of Christ in relation to the doctrine of justification. However, before proceeding, there is another element from the Genesis 15 narrative to consider.

Subsequent to his justification of Abraham, God made a covenant, an agreement, with the patriarch. In Abraham's day, it was typical for nations, clans, or individuals to make agreements, or covenants. Sometimes covenants were made between equals, or at other times there were covenants where one party was clearly more powerful than the other. Once the two parties agreed upon the terms of their covenant, the covenant was usually sealed with a ceremony. The two parties would take animals, cut them in half, and walk between the severed animal halves. The intention of the animal-cutting ceremony was to bind the two parties to their covenant agreement and commit to one another that if either party violated the terms of the covenant, then his fate would be the same as the severed animals (cf. Jer. 34:18–19). In the light of this information, we should take special note of what events transpire in this covenant-cutting ceremony between God and Abraham.

After God had Abraham cut the animals in two, the sun went down, and Abraham fell into a deep sleep (Gen. 15:9–12). Then a smoking fire pot and a flaming torch, symbolic images for the presence of God, passed between the severed animals alone. Significantly, God promises to Abraham that if the patriarch or God himself violates the terms of this covenant agreement, then God alone will bear the penalty for transgressing the covenant. Seeing that God cannot die, we also see the certainty that God will keep his promise. Once again, we find important elements of the doctrine of justification reemphasized here. Abraham is totally passive; he is in a deep sleep. It is God who is active, who makes the covenant promise, who justifies Abraham by imputing righteousness to him by faith, and who swears an immutable and unchanging covenant oath to bear any penalties for the covenant's violation. The promise that God made to Adam and Eve is slowly being revealed with increasing clarity here in the gospel covenant that God makes with Abraham. And it is on the heels of God passing between the severed animals that he makes his covenant oath to Abraham: "On that day the LORD made a covenant with Abram, saying, 'To your offspring I give this land'" (Gen. 15:18). The apostle Paul's commentary on this covenant promise proves to be immensely invaluable: "Now the promises were spoken to Abraham and to his seed. He does not say, 'And to seeds,' as referring to many, but rather to one, 'And to your seed,' that is, Christ" (Gal 3:16 NASB). Paul shows us that the covenant promise that God made to Abraham is fulfilled in Jesus Christ, God's only Son.

Summary

Thus far we have seen important points develop in the Genesis narrative. We have seen God place man in the garden and give him two commands: 1) not to eat from the tree of knowledge and 2) to fill the earth with the image of God and extend the garden-order to the ends of the earth. Adam failed. God re-created the earth and started over with a new "Adam," of sorts. Noah was a righteous man, yet he too failed to fulfill the command of filling the earth with the image of God. God therefore called Abraham, an ungodly man, and gave him a promise. What God had commanded Adam and Noah to do, he was now promising to give to Abraham and do through Abraham. Abraham believed this promise and was now righteous in the sight of God, not through his works or obedience, but by believing in the promise, by faith alone, in the gospel, the promise that the seed of the woman would conquer the seed of the serpent, and that God would give Abraham many offspring through his one seed, Jesus Christ. Moreover, Abraham's sinfulness no longer polluted him because God had credited or imputed righteousness to Abraham by faith. From where did this righteousness come? It was to come from God himself, God in the flesh, the promised seed of the woman, the seed of Abraham.

THE LIFE, DEATH, AND RESURRECTION OF JESUS

Fulfillment of the Law

Since the fall of the first man and woman, all of history waited in anticipation for the fulfillment of the promise of redemption. In the first century (AD) the time for God to fulfill his covenant promises had come. The gospels record the ministry of Christ, but it is a ministry that was rooted in the Old Testament. We see hints of these connections in the genealogies of Jesus, as Matthew identifies him as a descendant of Abraham and Luke as a descendant of Adam (Matt. 1:1; Luke 3:23–38). These genealogical connections are important, as they organically link Jesus to the promises of Genesis 3:15 and 15:18, the seed of the woman and the seed of Abraham. In this regard, Jesus was unique, as the gospel writers identify him as the fulfillment of God's redemptive promises. However, Christ's family tree was not all that made him unique.

In the gospel of Luke, the medical doctor turned theologian places the genealogy of Jesus between the account of his baptism and his wilderness wanderings. Christ's actions at this point are most certainly reminiscent of Israel's history. Israel was freed from Egypt in the miraculous exodus when they were delivered through the Red Sea crossing and led into the wilderness where they were to proceed to the Promised Land. The connections between Israel's history and Jesus' baptism and wilderness experience become clearer when we recall that God considered Israel to be his "firstborn son" (Ex. 4:22), that Paul called the Red Sea crossing a baptism (1 Cor. 10:1–2), and that Israel was led by the pillar of cloud by day and fire by night, identified by Isaiah as the Holy Spirit (Isa. 63:10–13; cf. Hag. 2:5). Now, however, Christ, the true Son of

God, emerged from the waters of baptism and had the Holy Spirit descend upon him and lead him into the wilderness like Israel of old. There was, of course, a big difference between Israel and Jesus. Old Testament Israel was rebellious, cantankerous, faithless, and above all else, disobedient. Jesus, unlike Adam, Noah, and Israel, was God's obedient, faithful, and submissive Son. He was the beloved Son in whom God the Father was well pleased (Luke 3:22). Christ's righteousness appears in his temptation in the wilderness. Israel wandered in the wilderness for forty years because of its disobedience. Jesus wandered in the wilderness for forty days, but when he was tempted, he was obedient.

In a well-known passage, Philippians 2:5–11, the apostle Paul extols the obedience of Jesus. But what is perhaps less familiar is that he does so by discreetly comparing Jesus to Adam. Paul writes that though Jesus "was in the form of God, [he] did not count equality with God a thing to be grasped," thus harkening back to Adam, who did try to grasp equality with God by taking of the forbidden fruit (Phil. 2:6). Paul tells us that, instead of trying to grasp equality with God, Jesus "made himself nothing, taking the form of a servant, being born in the likeness of men. And being found in human form, he humbled himself by becoming obedient to the point of death, even death on a cross" (Phil. 2:7–8). Here Paul lays great emphasis upon the obedience of Christ and hints at a comparison between the Messiah and Adam. Yet in two other passages Paul makes an explicit distinction between Jesus and Adam.

In Romans 5, Paul compares the respective work of Adam and Jesus. Paul begins by explaining what came about due to the sin of the first man, Adam: "Sin came into the world through one man, and death through sin, and so death spread to all men because all sinned" (Rom. 5:12). He then goes on to compare the results of Adam's sin and of Christ's obedience unto death: "The free gift is not like the result of that one man's sin. For the judgment following one trespass brought condemnation, but the free gift following many trespasses brought justification" (Rom. 5:16). Notice that Adam's sin brought condemnation upon all men, but by contrast the obedience of Christ brings justification:

> If, because of one man's trespass, death reigned through that one man, much more will those who receive the abundance of grace and the free gift of righteousness reign in life through the one man Jesus Christ. Therefore, as one trespass led to condemnation for all men, so one act of righteousness leads to justification and life for all men. For as by the one man's disobedience the many were made sinners, so by the one man's obedience the many will be made righteous. (Rom. 5:17–19)

Elsewhere Paul draws out the contrasting connections between Adam and Christ when he writes, "For as in Adam all die, so also in Christ shall all be made alive" (1 Cor. 15:22). Jesus therefore offers the obedience, the righteousness, that God required of man. In this way, the life of Christ is necessary for our justification. Here it is good to recall again the words of Horatius Bonar, "Thy works, not mine, O Christ, speak gladness to this heart; they tell me all is done; they bid my fear depart."

Paying the Penalty of the Law

Christ offered unto his heavenly Father the perfect obedience that no one else had been able to offer, whether before or after the fall. However, we must recognize that the penalty of disobeying God's command in the garden still hangs over the head of every man. Remember what Paul wrote about the sin of the first man: "Sin came into the world through one man, and death through sin, and so death spread to all men because all sinned" (Rom. 5:12). All people are credited, or imputed, with the sin of Adam, which brings both the guilt and pollution of sin. This means we are held accountable for Adam's sin as well as our own personal sins. It is this debt, so to speak, that Jesus came to pay—to remove the curse of the law that hung over the heads of those who had violated the law of God, whether Adam in the garden, Noah after the flood, or Israel in the Sinai wilderness and later in the Promised Land. In this regard Paul quite clearly states, "For all have sinned and fall short of the glory of God" (Rom. 3:23). Remember, though, it was God who passed through the severed animal halves and promised to bear the curse of the covenant.

In the epistle to the Galatian churches Paul explains the significance of the cross of Christ as it relates to our justification: "Christ redeemed us from the curse of the law by becoming a curse for us—for it is written, 'Cursed is everyone who is hanged on a tree'—so that in Christ Jesus the blessing of Abraham might come to the Gentiles, so that we might receive the promised Spirit through faith" (Gal. 3:13–14). Here Paul connects the covenant curse of being hung on a tree (Deut. 21:23) to the crucifixion of Christ. It is Christ who bore the curse of God; it was Jesus who suffered the wrath of God on our behalf so that we might have life. What we should realize, though, is that Christ suffered not only on the cross but also throughout his entire life. He suffered the insults and rejection of his people, was falsely accused of sin and blasphemy, and lived in austere conditions. He suffered all of these things because of the sin of Adam. But he also suffered all of these things, and especially upon the cross, a cruel instrument of torture and execution, so that those who look to Christ by faith do not have to suffer God's wrath. On the cross, Christ drank the cup of God's wrath on behalf of his bride, the church (Mark 14:36; cf. Rev. 16:19). So, then, the crucifixion of Christ is necessary for our justification. This is why Bonar writes, "Thy pains, not mine, O Christ, upon the shameful tree, have paid the law's full price and purchased peace for me."

Raised for Our Justification

The life and death of Christ are foundational to the doctrine of justification, but what many do not realize is that the resurrection is just as important and necessary. The resurrection is necessary for several reasons. First, if death was able to hold Jesus in its bonds, it would have meant that Jesus was guilty of sin. As Paul explains, "The wages of sin is death" (Rom. 6:23). Therefore, if Jesus had remained in the grave, his crucifixion would have been legitimate. Second, if Christ had not risen from the dead, it would have meant that the power of sin and death had not been broken and conquered. Third, if Jesus had not been raised from the dead, it would have meant that God had not accepted the sacrifice on behalf of the people of God. Paul explains to the Corinthians: "If Christ has not been raised, your faith is futile and you are still in your sins" (1 Cor. 15:17). It is for these three reasons, then, that Paul draws an intimate connection between the doctrine of justification and the resurrection of Jesus.

In Romans 4:25 Paul writes that Jesus was "delivered up for our trespasses and raised for our justification." In his crucifixion, Jesus pays the penalty for the violation of the law, but in his resurrection, the Father declares to the world that his Son is righteous and innocent of wrongdoing. Jesus breaks the power and bond of sin and death, and his Father announces to the world that the perfect sacrifice of his Son is accepted. It is in Christ's resurrection that we once again see the contrast of

the work of Adam and Jesus. In Adam, there is sin, condemnation, and eternal death, and in Jesus there is obedience, justification, and eternal life (cf. Dan. 12:2). Moreover, it is through
the resurrection of Jesus that he gives life through the outpour-
ing of the Holy Spirit upon his people, the church. In this regard Paul explains, "Thus it is written, 'The first man Adam
became a living being'; the last Adam became a life-giving
Spirit" (1 Cor. 15:45*). Here Paul quotes Genesis 2:7, which
tells of the creation of Adam, the first man, and contrasts it
with the work of the last Adam, Jesus, and shows how through
his resurrection he brings the renewing work of the Holy
Spirit. Paul goes on to elaborate the effects of the resurrection
of Christ when he writes: "The first man was from the earth, a
man of dust; the second man is from heaven. As was the man of
dust, so also are those who are of the dust, and as is the man of
heaven, so also are those who are of heaven. Just as we have
borne the image of the man of dust, we shall also bear the image of the man of heaven" (1 Cor. 15:47–49).

It is in this way that Christ's resurrection is necessary
for our justification. Geerhardus Vos, the well-known professor of biblical theology at Princeton seminary during the
late nineteenth- and early twentieth-century, colleague to Reformed greats such as B. B. Warfield, and professor to the likes
of J. Gresham Machen, explains: "We find in the resurrection
the strongest possible assurance of pardon and peace. When
Christ rose on Easter morning he left behind him in the depths
of the grave every one of our sins; there they remain buried
from the sight of God so completely that even in the day of
judgment they will not be able to rise up against us any more."[2]

Summary of the Work of Christ

We see that each part of Christ's work—his life, death, and
resurrection—are necessary for our justification. In his life,

Christ came to offer the obedience that no one had yet given to God, whether before the fall in the garden or after the fall. He offered this obedience throughout his life, which culminated in his crucifixion. In his death, Christ suffered the penalty of violating the law and bore the wrath of God on behalf of his people. And in the resurrection, the Father announced that his Son was righteous, that sin and death had been conquered, and that the Son's perfect sacrifice had been accepted. In these three things we see that it is the work of Christ that is foundational and the basis for our justification. It is not our obedience or good works that enable us to be justified in the sight of God. It is only the work of Christ (*solus Christus*) that is received through faith alone (*sola fide*) and by God's grace alone (*sola gratia*). It is Jesus who takes up the broken covenant of works and fulfills it. Jesus fulfills Genesis 1:28 and does so through the gospel (cf. Gen. 12:3; Matt. 28:18–19). In the end, we see Jesus as the last Adam who is surrounded by his offspring who bear his righteous image, who are robed in his righteousness, and who once again dwell in the presence of God (Rev. 21–22). Christ fills the earth with the glorious image of God through his work, not ours.

THE DOCTRINE OF JUSTIFICATION BY FAITH ALONE

In surveying the biblical data, we can summarize the key points of the doctrine of justification by faith alone:

- Justification is the legal declaration whereby God judges the one who looks to Christ by faith to be righteous in his sight.

- We must be justified by faith alone because, as a consequence of the indwelling presence of sin, we are incapable of offering to God the obedience he requires. Therefore, our faith is not introspective, looking within to see what we can do to save ourselves. Rather, our faith is extraspective, looking outside of ourselves to what Christ has done.

- The life, death, and resurrection of Christ are the foundation, the judicial ground, for our justification.
- Our justification by faith alone ensures our standing before God both in the present and in the future and guarantees that we have received eternal life.

Reflecting on this summary, it is critical that we recognize that the doctrine of justification by faith alone was the chief rallying cry of the sixteenth-century Reformation. While there were other theologians who laid the groundwork, Luther was the straw that broke the proverbial camel's back. One of Luther's contemporaries, a Roman Catholic priest by the name of Johann Tetzel, went about selling indulgences. An indulgence was supposed to be a "thank you," so to speak, for making a donation for the construction of St. Peter's cathedral in Rome. The pope dispensed these indulgences, supposedly to reduce the amount of time people would have to spend in purgatory or to free deceased relatives from purgatory. Tetzel coined the phrase "When the coin in the coffer rings, the soul from purgatory springs!" It was these events that finally lead Luther to pen his ninety-five theses and post them to the door of the Wittenberg castle on the eve of All Saints Day, October 31, 1517. With the recent invention of the printing press, Luther's theses were quickly copied and distributed throughout Europe, and in a short time the Reformation was born.

During the Reformation both Lutherans, those who followed Luther, and Reformed theologians, men such as Ulrich

Zwingli, John Calvin, Zacharias Ursinus, Heinrich Bullinger, Caspar Olevianus, and many others saw the truths that Luther expounded and agreed with them. Ultimately, they agreed with Luther because they recognized these truths to be the teaching of Scripture. The Reformers read the pages of Scripture, particularly the letters of Paul, and were convinced of the truth of justification by faith alone. These theologians saw to the codification of this doctrine in the confessions and catechisms of the Reformation.

In the following confessions and catechisms of the Reformation, we find affirmation of the doctrine of justification by faith alone.

Augsburg Confession (1530), Lutheran. "Our churches also teach that men cannot be justified before God by their own strength, merits, or works but are freely justified for Christ's sake through faith when they believe that they are received into favor and that their sins are forgiven through faith, when we believe that Christ suffered for us and that for his sake our sin is forgiven and righteousness and eternal life are given to us" (§ 4).

The French Confession (1559), French Reformed. "We believe that we are made partakers of this justification by faith alone, as it is written: 'He suffered for our salvation, that whosoever believes on him should not perish.' And this is done inasmuch as we appropriate to our use the promises of life which are given to us through him, and feel their effect when we accept them, being assured that we are established by the word of God and shall not be deceived. Thus our justification through faith depends upon the free promises by which God declares and testifies his love to us."

Belgic Confession (1561), Dutch Reformed. "We believe that our salvation consists in the remission of our sins for Jesus Christ's sake, and that therein our righteousness before God is implied; as David and Paul teach us, declaring this to be the happiness of man, that God imputes righteousness to him without works" (§ 23).

Heidelberg Catechism (1563), Dutch Reformed. "Q. Why sayest thou that thou art righteous by faith only? A. Not that I am acceptable to God, on account of the worthiness of my faith, but because only the satisfaction, righteousness, and holiness of Christ, is my righteousness before God; and that I cannot receive and apply the same to myself any other way than by faith only" (Q./A. 61).

Thirty-Nine Articles (1571), Anglican. "We are accounted righteous before God, only for the merit of our Lord and Savior Jesus Christ by faith, and not for our own works or deservings: Wherefore that we are justified by faith only is a most wholesome doctrine, and very full of comfort" (§ 11).

Westminster Confession of Faith (1647), Presbyterian; Second London Confession (1689), Baptist. "Faith, thus receiving and resting on Christ and his righteousness, is the alone instrument of justification" (§ 11.2).

By looking at this cross section of confessions and catechisms, both from the Reformation and post-Reformation periods, we can say that theologians across Europe from Germany, France, Holland, Scotland, and England and from a diverse body of churches—Lutheran, Reformed, Anglican, Baptist, and Presbyterian—all affirmed the doctrine of justification by faith alone. In this regard, the doctrine of justification by faith alone was not an obscure teaching limited only to small pockets of the world but was widely affirmed, taught, and confessed in sixteenth-century Europe and beyond. Before concluding, let us explore two questions that commonly arise in opposition to this doctrine.

ANSWERING OBJECTIONS

Antinomianism

Typically, two objections are raised when people hear about the biblical doctrine of justification by faith alone. The first objection is that such a teaching is dangerous and will lead people to live sinfully when they hear that their sins, past, present, and future, are forgiven when they place their faith in Christ. This type of reaction is born out of a fear of lawless living, or *antinomianism*. Without question there have always been those who, hearing the truth of the doctrine of justification, twist and abuse it. In fact, this is something that the apostle Paul himself faced. In his letter to Rome, Paul answers the question "Are we to continue in sin that grace may abound?" (Rom. 6:1). In other words, there were some who thought that "If God is in the business of forgiving sins, and I'm a sinner, then we have a perfect arrangement. I can sin, and God will forgive me by his grace." To this erroneous response to the doctrine of justification Paul gave his unqualified "By no means" (Rom. 6:2)!

Paul explains that through our justification by faith alone, there is a break with our old existence in Adam as we are brought to life in Christ Jesus. Paul writes, "Do you not know that all of us who have been baptized into Christ Jesus were baptized into his death? We were buried therefore with him by baptism into death, in order that, just as Christ was raised from the dead by the glory of the Father, we too might walk in newness of life" (Rom. 6:3–4). We see that our justification by faith effects a definitive break with our sinful existence in Adam and begins our new existence in Christ. Elsewhere, Paul explains that connected to the blessing of God's grace in justification is the transforming work of the Holy Spirit: "Christ redeemed us from the curse of the law by becoming a curse for us—for it is written, 'Cursed is everyone who is hanged on a tree'—so that in Christ Jesus the blessing of Abraham might come to the Gentiles, *so that we might receive the promised Spirit through faith*" (Gal. 3:13–14). Here we find that a correlative blessing of justification is the indwelling work of the Holy Spirit. And it is later in his letter to the Galatians where Paul writes that the Holy Spirit produces his fruit within us: love, joy, peace, patience, kindness, goodness, gentleness, faithfulness, and self-control (Gal. 5:22–23).

Being justified through faith alone and being united to Christ, the believer at the same time is inhabited by the Holy Spirit, who produces in the believer the holiness and righteousness of Christ. This transformative process where the believer is conformed to the image of Christ is called *sanctification*. This means everyone who is justified by faith alone is also being sanctified. That is, they become more and more righteous, not more sinful. Calvin explains that by partaking of Christ "we principally receive a double grace: namely, that being reconciled to God through Christ's blamelessness, we may have in heaven instead of a Judge a gracious Father; and secondly, that sanctified by Christ's spirit we may cultivate blamelessness and purity of life."[3] To this end, it is important that we see what the Westminster Confession says about the double grace of justification and sanctification: "Faith, thus receiving and resting on Christ and his righteousness, is the alone instrument of justification: yet is it not alone in the person justified, but is ever accompanied with all other saving graces, and is no dead faith, but works by love" (11.2). In other words, the believer who is united to Christ by faith is justified, and that union with Christ produces the fruit of holiness, or good works. The believer's good works are not the cause of his justification, but rather the effect.

Legalism

Another common objection is that the doctrine of justification by faith alone seems too good to be true: "How can we receive the forgiveness of sins, the imputation of righteousness, and not contribute in any way to our salvation?" Again, this is a problem that the apostle Paul faced in his own ministry. Paul planted a number of churches in the province of Galatia. Shortly after his departure, false teachers came into the churches and began to teach that the Gentile Christians not only had to believe in Jesus Christ but also had to be circumcised in order to be saved. The false teachers taught that a person was justified and saved by faith plus works—in this case, faith plus circumcision. This type of response is a form of *legalism*, believing that the Christian can somehow obtain God's favor through his obedience. Paul's response to this teaching was powerful and swift, as he called it a false gospel (Gal. 1:8–9). Paul rebuked the Galatians by asking them, "Did you receive the Spirit by works of the law or by hearing with faith? Are you so foolish? Having begun by the Spirit, are you now being perfected by the flesh?" (Gal. 3:2–3). What the legalist often does not realize is that the law of God is powerless to save; it only has the power to condemn. This is why we must look to Jesus by faith: "We know that a person is not justified by works of the law but through faith in Jesus Christ, so we also have believed in Christ Jesus, in order to be justified by faith in Christ and not by works of the law, because by works of the law no one will be justified. . . . I do not nullify the grace of God, for if justification were through the law, then Christ died for no purpose" (Gal. 2:16, 21; cf. Rom. 2–3).

When people hear the gospel, which at its heart is the doctrine of justification by faith alone, and they think it is too good to be true, it is only then that they have begun to plumb the depths of God's love for us in Christ. In the doctrine of justification by faith alone, we must realize that legalism is a poor substitute for the all-sufficient work of Christ. How can the believer add to the already perfect and sufficient work of Christ? God's grace is, as the famous hymn says, amazing!

CONCLUSION

Before concluding, we should make several observations regarding what one might call the practical implications of the doctrine of justification. First, we should realize that no biblical doctrine is impractical, let alone the doctrine of justification. What could be more practical and relevant than Jesus Christ stepping into the breach between sinful man and a holy God, offering the obedience that God requires, suffering his wrath, and being raised so that we might have eternal life and dwell in the presence of the triune Lord? Nothing could be more practical than redemption from the just, eternal wrath of God. In addition to this wonderful blessing, there are a host of other attendant blessings that accompany the truths of the doctrine of justification by faith alone. Paul tells us, for example, "Therefore, since we have been justified by faith, we have peace with God through our Lord Jesus Christ" (Rom. 5:1). In other words, we can have peace and assurance in our souls because we no longer know God as our judge but instead know him as our heavenly Father because of the work of our older brother, Jesus Christ (cf. Col. 1:15; Heb. 2:10–18). The believer no longer has to bear the guilt and shame of sin, because Christ has borne it for him.

Moreover, we can also rest assured that nothing can separate us from the love of God that is in Christ Jesus—not Satan, not the unbelieving world, not even our own sin. As Paul wrote to the church in Rome, "Who shall bring any charge against God's elect? It is God who justifies. Who is to condemn? Christ Jesus is the one who died—more than that, who was raised—who is at the right hand of God, who indeed is interceding for us" (Rom. 8:33–34). Therefore, for the one who mourns over his sin and carries about the dreadful load of oppressive guilt, there is freedom, joy, and happiness, because Christ has borne that awful load on his behalf. For the parents who mourn as they watch their covenant child descend into a self-destructive pattern of sin, there is hope, hope that God can open their child's eyes to repent and look to Jesus by faith and receive his imputed righteousness.

It is the doctrine of justification by faith alone that brought hope to Adam and Eve as they trembled in God's presence, to Moses when he sinned and was barred from entering the Promised Land, to David when he fell into grave sin with Bathsheba, to Paul when he realized that he was persecuting the bride of Christ, and to every person whose eyes God has opened so they might realize their sin and see that the only remedy for their hopeless condition is in the life, death, and resurrection of Christ, received by faith alone. Truly, the doctrine of justification is the main hinge upon which religion turns and is indeed the article upon which the church stands or falls!

N**OTE**S

1 John Calvin, *Institutes of the Christian Religion*, ed. John T. McNeill, trans. Ford Lewis Battles (Philadelphia: Westminster Press, 1960), 3.11.1.

2 Geerhardus Vos, *Grace and Glory: Sermons Preached in the Chapel of Princeton Theological Seminary* (Edinburgh: Banner of Truth Trust, 1994), 161–62.

3 Calvin, *Institutes*, 3.11.1.